S0-ARO-633

Pets at My House

Turtles

Jennifer Blizin Gillis

Heinemann Library
Chicago, Illinois

© 2004 Heinemann Library
a division of Reed Elsevier Inc.
Chicago, Illinois

Customer Service   888–454–2279
Visit our website at www.heinemannlibrary.com

Page layout by Kim Kovalick, Heinemann Library
Printed and bound in China by South China Printing Company Limited.
Photo research by Jill Birschbach

08 07 06 05 04
10 9 8 7 6 5 4 3 2 1
Library of Congress Cataloging-in-Publication Data

Gillis, Jennifer Blizin, 1950-
Turtles / Jennifer Blizin Gillis.
      p. cm. -- (Pets at my house)
   ISBN 1-4034-5056-0 (hardcover) -- ISBN 1-4034-6023-X (pbk.)
   1. Turtles as pets--Juvenile literature. 2. Painted turtle--Juvenile literature. I. Title. II. Series.
   SF459.T8G568 2004
   639.3'92--dc22

                                   2004003196

Acknowledgments

The author and publishers are grateful to the following for permission to reproduce copyright material:

Cover photograph by Robert Pickett/Papilio
p. 4, 18 Robert Lifson/Heinemann Library; p. 5 Heinemann Library; p. 6l Royalty-free/Corbis; pp. 6r, 9, 16, 20 Robert Pickett/Papilio; p. 7 Arbdt/Premium Stock/Picture Quest; pp. 8, 10 Robert Maier/Animals Animals; p. 11 Trevor Clifford/Heinemann Library; pp. 12, 14, 19 Tudor Photography/Heinemann Library; p. 13 David Young-Wolff/Photo Edit; p. 15 Jorg & Petra Wegner/Animals Animals; p. 17 Dave Bradford/Heinemann Library; pp. 21, 22 PhotoDisc/Getty Images; p. 23 (from T-B) Arndt/Premium Stock/PictureQuest, Royalty-Free/Corbis, Photodisc/Getty Images, Photodisc/Getty Images, Robert Maier/Animals Animals, Heinemann Library, Heinemann Library; back cover (L-R) Robert Maier/Animals Animals, David Young-Wolff/Photo Edit

Every effort has been made to contact copyright holders of any material reproduced in this book. Any omissions will be rectified in subsequent printings if notice is given to the publisher.

Special thanks to our advisory panel for their help in the preparation of this book:

Alice Bethke,
Library Consultant
Palo Alto, CA

Eileen Day,
Preschool Teacher
Chicago, IL

Kathleen Gilbert,
Second Grade Teacher
Round Rock, TX

Sandra Gilbert,
Library Media Specialist
Fiest Elementary School
Houston, TX

Jan Gobeille, Kindergarten Teacher
Garfield Elementary
Oakland, CA

Angela Leeper,
Educational Consultant
Wake Forest, NC

Contents

Some words are shown in bold, **like this.**
You can find them in the picture glossary on page 23.

What Kind of Pet Is This?

Pets are animals that live with us.

Some pets are small and furry.

Painted turtle

Our pet is small and has a
hard shell.

Can you guess what kind of pet
this is?

What Are Painted Turtles?

carapace

plastron

Turtles are **reptiles**.

Turtles have two shells called a **carapace** and a **plastron**.

Painted turtles have a green shell with colored markings.

Their plastrons are red.

Where Did My Turtle Come From?

A mother turtle laid eggs in a **nest**.

When the eggs hatched, **hatchlings** came out.

The hatchlings grew to be about as big as a biscuit.

Then I bought one at the pet store.

How Big Is My Turtle?

At first, my turtle was as big as the end of your finger.

Now it is as big as a dinner plate.

In the wild, painted turtles do not grow as big.

This is because they do not live as long as turtles kept as pets.

Where Does My Turtle Live?

aquarium

Painted turtles spend most of their time in water.

They need an **aquarium** with a pond to swim in.

In warm weather, painted turtles can live outside near a pond.

They need to have dirt and leaves nearby to hide or sleep in.

What Does My Turtle Eat?

Turtles eat vegetables like carrots and lettuce.

They eat pond plants, too.

In the wild, turtles eat bugs
and worms.

At home, my turtle eats dry
turtle food.

What Else Does My Turtle Need?

Turtles need to lie in the sun to keep warm.

So, my **aquarium** has a light that shines on my turtle.

Outside, I need to keep my turtle safe from other animals.

Raccoons and dogs are a danger to turtles.

What Can I Do for My Turtle?

I keep my turtle's home clean.

I wash its **aquarium** with soap and water.

I put **calcium** on my turtle's food.

This helps keep its shell strong and hard.

What Can My Turtle Do?

Some people call painted turtles sliders.

When the turtles see something moving, they slide into the water.

Outside, my turtle can easily hide.

Its markings help it blend into leaves and bushes.

Turtle Map

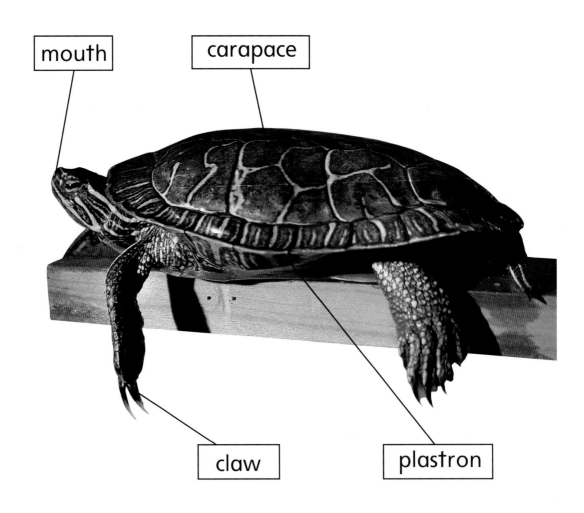

mouth

carapace

claw

plastron

Picture Glossary

aquarium
pages 12, 16, 18
kind of box with glass sides where turtles, fish, or other pets can live

calcium
page 19
something that can make bones, teeth, and turtle shells hard

carapace
page 6
top part of a turtle's shell

hatchlings
pages 8, 10
young turtles that have just come out of an egg

nest
page 8
place an animal digs or builds for its eggs

plastron
pages 6, 7
bottom part of a turtle's shell

reptile
page 6
animal with scales or a shell, and that needs heat from the sun to stay warm

Note to Parents and Teachers

Reading for information is an important part of a child's literacy development. Learning begins with a question about something. Help children think of themselves as investigators and researchers by encouraging their questions about the world around them. Each chapter in this book begins with a question. Read the question together. Look at the pictures. Talk about what you think the answer might be. Then read the text to find out if your predictions were correct. Think of other questions you could ask about the topic, and discuss where you might find the answers. Assist children in using the picture glossary and the index to practice new vocabulary and research skills.

❗ CAUTION: Remind children to be careful when handling animals. Pets may scratch or bite if startled. Children should wash their hands with soap and water after they touch any animal.

Index